Kicking the Football Soccer Style

GW00778039

PETE GOGOLAK

EDITED BY RAY SIEGENER

Kicking the Football Soccer Style

AN ALADDIN BOOK
Atheneum

PHOTOGRAPHS BY RAY SIEGENER AND BY
COURTESY OF THE NEW YORK COSMOS

PUBLISHED BY ATHENEUM
COPYRIGHT © 1972 BY PETE GOGOLAK AND RAY SIEGENER
ALL RIGHTS RESERVED
PUBLISHED SIMULTANEOUSLY IN CANADA BY
MCCLELLAND & STEWART LTD.
MANUFACTURED IN THE UNITED STATES OF AMERICA BY
THE MURRAY PRINTING COMPANY,
FORGE VILLAGE, MASSACHUSETTS
ISBN 0-689-70406-2
FIRST ALADDIN EDITION

Contents

Kicking the Football
Soccer Style

1. I Get a Kick Out of Kicking

THIS KIND of situation could happen on almost any Sunday in the life of a place kicker:

Time was running out for the New York Giants. The score was 21 to 21, and my team, the Giants, needed a win over the Dallas Cowboys to stay out in front in our division. On third down our quarterback, Fran Tarkenton, dropped back to throw, but the pass rush was on. Bob Lilly, the Cowboy's all-pro defensive tackle, broke through the wall of blockers and almost caught Fran behind the line of scrimmage. Tarkenton had to throw quickly, and the ball sailed out of bounds just inches from the outstretched hands of flanker Cliff McNeil.

The clock stopped with just five seconds to go. The ball was on the forty-one-yard line—forty-eight yards from the goal post. I could feel the ten-

sion in my stomach as I waited for Coach Alex
Webster to call for the kicking unit. This was it—
the moment that every place kicker waits for and
dreads. Bullfighters call it the moment of truth.
Suddenly you are the most important man on the
team.

But as I fastened my chin strap and trotted out
onto the field, the tension faded away. My mind
was checking the situation. The ball was on the
forty-one-yard line—add the seven yards between
the goal line and posts and the kick would have to
carry forty-eight yards. A pretty long attempt. The
surface of the field was dry and firm. The wind
was blowing almost straight in from the open end
of Yankee Stadium. It would help the kick. The
angle was good . . . almost straightaway.

We broke the huddle, and Tarkenton, who used
to hold the ball for me on field goal attempts, positioned himself seven yards behind the ball. As I
looked past Fran at those distant uprights, I said to
myself, "Relax, Peter, just keep your eye on the
ball and forget those Dallas linemen." Luckily,
you don't have too much time to think out there.
Suddenly the ball was centered back by Greg Lar-

sen. Fran coolly positioned the ball with the laces away from the point of impact. I whipped my leg into the ball and followed through. The kick felt good. The ball sailed cleanly through the uprights and just cleared the crossbar. Fifty thousand Giant fans were whooping and hollering ecstatically; but no one felt more like shouting for joy than Peter Gogolak.

That's what it's all about when you're a place kicker. But it takes a lot of hard training and lonely hours of practice to prepare a kicker for that situation where he comes into the game and kicks the winning field goal with only seconds on the clock. This is one of the most exciting moments in sports, and it belongs to the place kicker.

One of the great things about place kicking is that any boy can do it. A boy's size is not important. Speed is not a factor. I suppose that there are certain qualities that a boy should have if he wants to become a kicker. But these qualities are not physical; they have more to do with personality and attitude.

Most kickers I know seem to be people who are

individuals in the true sense of the word. Kickers have to be able to practice by themselves. In fact, many kickers have to learn to kick by themselves. This is because good coaching in place kicking is not always available to boys playing for high school and sandlot football teams. A boy who wants to become a kicker must face the fact that the coach will be spending most of his time with the rest of the team. He will be teaching the team the strategy of the game. He will be supervising drills in blocking and tackling. He will be working with his backs and pass receivers.

One of the reasons that I have written this book is so that you can learn the fundamentals of place kicking by yourself if necessary. Then you can approach your coach and show him what you can do . . . how you can make an important contribution to the team. Let me give you an example.

When I first went to Cornell, kicking was not a very important part of the team's football strategy. As a matter of fact, in ten years, from 1950 to 1960, the Cornell team had kicked only three field goals.

I came to Cornell as a soccer-style kicker. You

6

can imagine how a lot of people felt about that. No one had ever heard of a soccer-style kicker before. I was the first kicker to introduce this technique into college ball and later into professional football. In my first game as a freshman, I had my chance to show what a place kicker could contribute to the team. Our team was playing the Yale freshmen. We hadn't beaten them in five years. I kicked three field goals and an extra point in that game. We won 16 to 10, and that was when I first realized what great potential there was for me as a place kicker. I had made a wise decision in becoming a kicking specialist.

I remember one game early in my pro career that brought this home to me. It was Thanksgiving Day in 1964. The Buffalo Bills, my first pro team, were playing the Chargers in San Diego. It was late in the game, the score was 24 to 24, and we had to win that one to make it into the play-offs. The game was being nationally televised, so the pressure was really on when they called for the kicking unit. This was a tough spot for a first-year man, especially since I had missed a field goal in the first half. On that first attempt, Ernie Ladd, who is about six foot nine inches tall and weighs about three hundred and twenty pounds, had come crashing in to try to block the kick. I had made the mistake of looking up, and there he was, looming up in front of me like a mountain. I missed that first goal by about twenty yards. Now that the score was tied and the clock was running out, I couldn't afford to miss again. Fortunately, I made the crucial kick, a thirty-four yarder, and we won the game 27 to 24.

I cite these instances because, for a place kicker, there's no feeling in the world that compares with the moment when the ball goes through the uprights. And that is a thrill that any boy can experience if he has the desire to be a place kicker. As I mentioned before, size is not important. For example, my brother Charlie, who plays for the Patriots, is only five foot nine and weighs one hundred sixty pounds, yet he has had a very successful professional career. And look at the great little place kicker with the Miami Dolphins, Garo Yepremian, who is only five foot eight and weighs only one hundred and fifty-five pounds. In the 1971 play-off game with the Kansas City Chiefs—the longest pro football game ever played—Yepremian outkicked the Chief's Jon Stenarud and scored the tie-breaking points. Maybe the best example of all is Tom Dempsey, of the Philadelphia Eagles. Tom, who plays wearing a special orthopedic shoe, overcame severe physical handicaps just to become a professional football player. In 1970, against the Detroit Lions, he set the record for the longest field goal in pro football history—sixty-three yards.

No matter how big or small you are, you can become a good place kicker if you really want to. Place kicking appeals to boys who are individualists because it is a very individual talent. It is truly doing your own thing. Let's face it: you will have the cleanest uniform on the team and the rest of the guys are going to kid you about it. You will have to practice by yourself. You will have to develop your own technique, unless you are lucky enough to have an experienced kicker to coach you. Then, in the game, you will have to go out there on the field and put the ball through the uprights . . . by yourself. Yet, at that moment, you will be very much a part of the team.

2. Soccer-Style or Conventional Kicking?

WHEN I was a boy I lived in Hungary. Like most other European boys, I grew up with a soccer ball always close to my feet. In almost every country other than the United States, you see youngsters dribbling soccer balls down the street and passing them back and forth to one another. They do this wherever they go, and, of course, they become very proficient at kicking the ball and controlling it with their feet. Now I am beginning to see the same thing happening in America. Elementary schools, high schools, and colleges all over the country are fielding soccer teams. I will have a good deal more to say about the game of soccer in later chapters of this book.

More and more soccer-style kickers are coming into professional football and are impressing coaches with the distance they can kick the football. People like Garo Yepremian, of the Miami Dolphins, Jon Stenarud, of the Kansas City Chiefs, and Horst Muhlmann, of the Cincinnati Bengals, consistently score with long field goal attempts. In fact, the New York Jets traded a high-scoring place kicker, Jim Turner, for British soccer-style kicker Bobby Howfield. The reason the Jets wanted Howfield was because of his ability to get more distance on kickoffs. I personally believe that the soccer-style kicker can achieve an average of six to eight yards over the conventional straight-away kicker.

I am often asked why soccer-style kickers seem to be able to kick the football greater distances. I have several theories about this. Most of us in professional football who kick soccer style have had a considerable soccer background. In the game of soccer, you not only kick the ball, but you also run constantly. This builds up the leg muscles. You simply can't be a soccer player without developing powerful legs, so one advantage the soccer-style kickers have is that they are apt to bring a stronger leg into the game.

As for the kick itself, I believe that the soccer technique lends itself to more power. The conventional kicker punches at the ball with his foot. The soccer kick involves the entire body. To explain this, I like to compare the soccer kick with the golf swing. A good golfer winds his body like a spring as he goes into his backswing. He then whips the clubhead through the ball in a powerful unwinding action. His follow-through helps him to keep his body, his hands, and the club face in position to ensure an accurate shot.

We will be taking a step-by-step look at the soccer kick in Chapter Four, and you will see how the kicker uses these same principles. Ben Hogan, one of America's all-time greatest golf pros and one of the finest teachers of the game, emphasizes what he calls the "inside muscles." He points out that the muscles of the torso and the inside of the thighs are keys to a powerful golf swing. These same muscles come into play in the soccer kick much more than in the straightaway kick.

I should make a very important point here. I

have been emphasizing the advantages of soccer-style kicking over the conventional, straightaway method. This is the way I kick, and I truly believe that it is the superior way. But the important thing should be place kicking itself. Whether you kick soccer style or straightaway is not going to make a tremendous amount of difference. Tom Dempsey, of the Philadelphia Eagles, who holds the professional record of sixty-three yards, is a conventional kicker. Kicking is like anything else. If you pick a style that suits you, and you learn it well, you can be a standout performer. For this reason, I am including in this book a section on conventional kicking. If you find that soccer-style kicking is difficult for you, don't allow that to stop you from becoming a place kicker. All of the rewards of kicking that I mentioned in Chapter One are there for the place kicker, whichever style he uses.

3. Training and Preparation for the Season

ANY BOY who has ideas about becoming an athlete is going to hear a lot about physical fitness, conditioning, and training. Sometimes we tend to look upon these things as the price we have to pay to excel in sports. However, I believe that most successful athletes have another way of looking at conditioning. They have experienced the sheer pleasure of being healthy, well-conditioned people. Being physically sound is very satisfying and helps to build confidence.

One of the things a good athlete does is find ways that are fun to keep himself in shape. Running is the best conditioner I know of. But unless you are on the track team at school, you may not enjoy running enough for it to be an effective way to condition your body. Why not combine your running with something that is fun . . . like basketball? If you get a regular diet of basketball, you are going to be in good shape for football, especially kicking. The benefits of a game such as basketball are obvious. It is good for your wind, it helps to develop sharp reflexes, and it keeps your legs in good condition.

A game that is even better for conditioning a kicker is soccer. Soccer provides you with plenty of kicking practice. It also builds up the muscles that you will need for place kicking when the football season approaches. Games such as basketball and soccer have another common benefit. They are both fast-moving games that force a boy to make quick, accurate decisions under the stress of competition. You may not see how this ability can help a place kicker, but there are times when it will. Many unforeseen things happen on a football field during a game. A bad snap from center, for example, may place you in the new role of running back or passer.

Remember, although your specific goal may be

to become a place kicker, your overall objective should be that of becoming a good athlete. If you are athletically inclined, then you probably enjoy playing any sport; and all sports—especially running sports—will help your legs and general physical condition.

Your physical education instructor or coach will be glad to advise you on conditioning. He knows what exercises and calisthenics are suitable for your age and build. I have been impressed by the physical fitness programs available at many schools. A large number of schools are using the exercises programs designed by the President's Council on Physical Fitness. These exercises are scientifically selected so that they build all-around fitness. They condition all of the major muscle groups, they strengthen the heart and respiratory system, and they even improve posture. This kind of conditioning will help your performance on the field. I am always surprised at the poor condition of some of the young men that show up at the training camps of the professional football teams. It is tough for a man who has his heart set on a pro football career to be released from camp by the second or third day simply because he has not bothered to keep himself in shape.

If you are already on a team as a kicker, you should be getting in some practice during the off season. My advice is not to kick too often—no more, say, than twice a week. Get a kicking tee and a ball and work mainly on meeting the ball properly and following through. Once again, your main goal during the off-season should be keeping your legs strong and your body in good shape. I say enjoy the summer: swim, play basketball, play soccer, ride your bike, and do all of the active things that you like to do. These things should have you in pretty good shape when the football season rolls around.

4. First Approach to Kicking

BOYS WHO have been playing soccer in school or on a team will have a head start when it comes to kicking the football soccer style. For the rest of you, the soccer kick will be a new challenge.

Kicking the football soccer style means doing some things differently than you would if you were kicking straightaway. First, the soccer-style kicker lines up differently. He doesn't stand directly behind the ball but approaches it from an angle. His leg motion is different. The conventional kicker brings his foot straight back, then drives it forward through the ball. The soccer-style kicker sweeps his leg through an arc rather than a straight line as he drives through the ball.

Another difference is the point of contact where

the foot meets the ball. I kick the ball high up on the inside of my foot—my instep—in the area of the laces on my shoes, while the conventional kicker strikes the ball with his toes.

I know that by now you are anxious to get started as a kicker. All you will need at this point are a ball, a pair of football shoes, and a kicking tee. I have a couple of suggestions about each of these items.

You can use just about any football to begin your kicking practice. Younger boys may find that at first a light ball or a junior-sized ball will be easier for them to kick than a regulation-sized ball. But remember, kicking puts a lot of wear and tear on a ball. A very inexpensive ball will not hold up long under the punishment of kicking.

When you purchase your football shoes, it is advisable to get a pair with interchangeable cleats. Your kicking shoe should have the shortest cleats available. A soccer-style kicker must get his foot well under the ball without his cleats catching on the turf. The soccer-style kicker has to be especially conscious of his left foot (or his right foot,

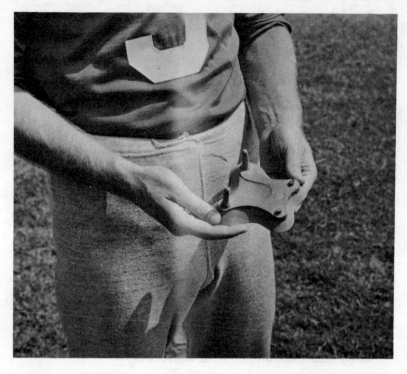

A close-up of standard kicking tee.

if he kicks with his left). Because of the action of the hips and legs, which I will explain later, the left foot must be firmly anchored to the ground. You can experiment with different-length cleats. Just remember that on a muddy or soft surface you should use longer cleats on your left shoe.

When we play on synthetic surfaces such as Astroturf, we use special shoes that have about twenty small cleats on them. These are specially designed for artificial surfaces. I use one of these shoes on my left foot and my regular kicking shoe on my right.

Conventional kickers use a regular-cleated shoe on the left foot (or right foot, if they kick left-footed) and a kicking shoe with a square toe on the kicking foot.

It is a good idea for you to learn how to tape your ankles for extra support. You can use an elastic-type bandage for this purpose. Give extra attention to your left foot, but don't put the tape on too tight.

When you go to the sporting goods store to buy a kicking tee, ask the salesman if he has different

Select a spot where the ground is flat and dry to place the kicking tee.

Set the ball on the tee so that it is almost vertical, pointed back slightly. The laces must face away from the area where the foot will meet the ball.

These photographs show how the broad surface of the high instep contacts the football.

types of tees. Tell him to help you select a tee that will elevate the toe of the ball off the ground as much as possible. You will be able to use almost any standard kicking tee; but an elevated tee will help you to get your foot under the ball.

TEEING UP THE BALL

When you take your ball and kicking tee out to an open practice area, select a tree or other suitable landmark as a target. (You don't need goal posts yet, but you do need some target so that you can set up your angle of approach to the ball and also so that you can tell if your kicks are going in the correct general direction.) Set your ball up on the tee with the laces facing the target.

STANCE

It is best to begin with a two-step kick. A two-step kick means a one-step approach and kicking on the second step. To assume the correct stance for a two-step kick, you should first stand directly behind the ball so that you are looking right over the ball at your target. The purpose of the target in the beginning is to help you line up correctly and to judge the line of your kicks.

Now move around to your left so that you are about thirty degrees off a straight line from ball to target. This is an approximate position. The angle of approach varies somewhat among soccer-style kickers. If you are confused about the thirty-degree angle after you have looked at the diagram, ask your father or your coach to help you. You should be facing the ball, with your left foot about one step away from it. Your right foot should be about one half step in front of your left foot.

Before you begin your approach, you should lean forward from the waist. Relax your body as much as possible, with your arms hanging loosely at your sides. Your eyes and your total attention should be fixed upon the ball. Keep your eyes on the ball throughout the approach right up to impact.

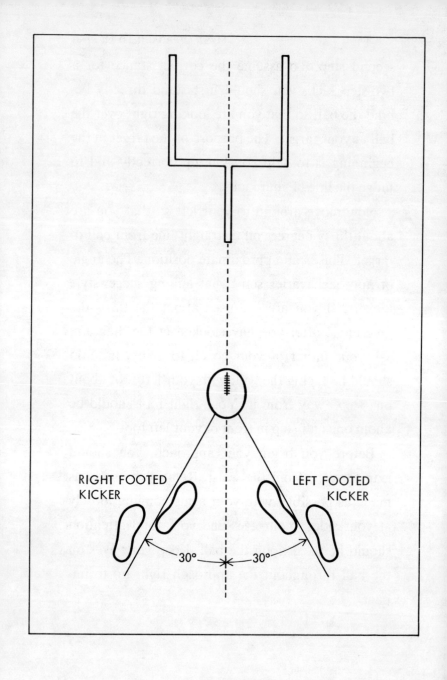

RIGHT FOOTED
KICKER

LEFT FOOTED
KICKER

30° 30°

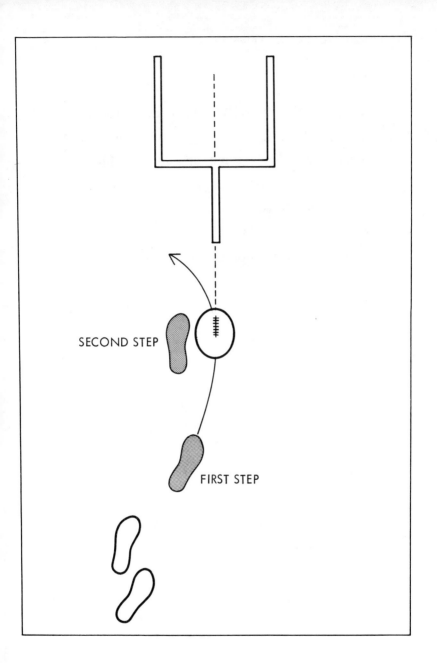

SECOND STEP

FIRST STEP

APPROACH

Most boys instinctively want to run at the ball before they kick it. I am going to recommend only a one-step approach at first, and you may find that it feels unnatural, or uncomfortable. A one-step approach means you take one step, then kick. The kick is your second step.

The one-step approach will help you learn to meet the ball properly with your right foot. This is the key now. If you are going to be a soccer-style kicker, the following points are very important, but not difficult.

Your first action in a one-step approach is to step off with your left foot. This first step should position your left foot right alongside the ball—about a foot away from it. As you take this first step, rotate your left foot so that when you plant it, it points directly at your target. This starts a rotating action of your hips, and this, in turn, creates the sweep or arc of your right leg.

I find that I can maintain my balance by extending my left arm straight out from my body as I approach the ball. My right arm is not ex-

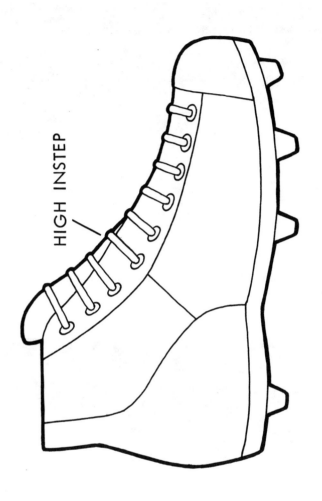

HIGH INSTEP

THE TWO-STEP KICK *I set myself up one long stride behind the ball.
My right foot is slightly ahead of my left.*

My left arm extends for balance as I begin my first step . . .

. . . which plants my left foot alongside the ball.

I drive my right foot through the ball, and follow through.

tended as fully. When you attempt a two-step kick, do not worry about cocking your right leg back fully. Your main objective will be to meet the ball correctly.

CONTACTING THE BALL

Tee your football up and try a two-step kick. Your foot should contact the ball on the high instep. This area of the foot will deliver maximum control and impact to the kick. Study the photos and drawings carefully, so that you are sure that you know exactly where the impact area is.

Try a couple of kicks to get the feel of it. You have to get your foot well under the ball in order to make contact on the high instep. When you do this correctly, you will find that you can get the ball up in the air. Be sure to keep your toe down and your foot extended as you come into the ball.

FOLLOW-THROUGH

As a young athlete, you are going to hear one bit

of advice over and over again. Whether you are throwing a football or kicking one, whether you are bowling or hitting a golf ball, the follow-through is a key factor. Follow-through helps keep all the other actions in the kick under control. This is because a correct follow-through is impossible if any of the key parts of the kick are done incorrectly.

Right up to the moment that you contact the ball, you should be bent forward slightly at the waist. As you bring your leg through the ball, your body straightens up. Your right leg swings up to the left of your target, with the toe of your kicking foot extended or pointed straight out. If you have done everything smoothly without rushing or trying to kick too hard, you will be comfortably balanced on your left foot. Here is a simple illustration of the two-step soccer-style kick.

I would advise you to spend a couple of days using the two-step method. Do this until you can consistently meet the ball with the proper part of the foot. Don't worry about distance yet. Just try to get the ball up in the air in the general direction of your target. And don't forget to follow

THE THREE-STEP KICK *I set up one step farther back. My left foot is slightly ahead of my right.*

The first step is with my right foot. Note my concentration on the ball.

I begin my second step, which will place my left foot alongside the ball.

My right foot contacts the ball on the high instep. My eyes are still on the ball.

A good follow-through, indicating good balance.

through. In other words, try to get the "feel" of a good kick.

THE THREE-STEP KICK

In order to generate the power necessary for most field goals, you have to develop some momentum by taking an extra step. The three-step kick gives you a running start and helps introduce body action into the kick. By getting the whole body behind the kick, the place kicker can get more power than with just his leg.

When you begin to feel comfortable with the two-step kick and are ready to add a little distance, you should advance to the three-step kick. A three-step kick requires a two-step approach; you kick on the third step. You will have to experiment a little to find the best distance for you to stand from the ball. This really depends on the length of your steps. For extra points and most field goals, I take two short, quick steps and kick on the third step. For very long field goals that require maximum power, I set up slightly farther back and increase the length of my stride as I approach.

To set up for a three-step kick, face the ball from a thirty-degree angle just as you did before. Now you can stand with your left foot forward rather than your right. (Remember: just the opposite for lefties.) Once again, fix your eyes on the ball and keep them there throughout the entire kick. Your first step is with your right foot. Your second step plants your left foot alongside the ball. Remember to rotate your left foot so that it is pointing at the target. This is the trigger that begins the arcing sweep of your right leg.

As you go into the second step, cock your right leg back. If you look carefully at the sequence photos, you will see the timing of these actions. When you kick, try to develop a nice easy rhythm. From here on it is just the same as the two-step kick, except your leg will deliver more power. Contact the ball with the high instep. Then complete the follow-through with your leg straight, and toe pointed straight out and your body upright.

CORRECTING BAD KICKS

Most boys who attempt soccer-style kicking for the first time find that the ball either pulls off to the left, or else the kick is too low, or both of these things happen. Because of a strong natural tendency to kick the ball with your toe, you must remember to keep the toe pointed down when your foot comes into the ball. This will allow you to get your foot well under the ball so that the point of impact is the high instep. When you do this correctly, the ball will fly high and far. A kick that hooks off to the left is caused by improper balance at the moment of impact. Because your body is in an unstable attitude, your foot hooks the ball and pulls it to the left instead of driving it straight toward the target. Here is a list of the most common causes for a bad kick:

(1) *Taking your eyes off the ball.* This will often cause you to contact the ball in the wrong place or with the wrong part of the foot.

(2) *Rushing the kick.* Rushing the kick will break your rhythm and cause you to lose accuracy, power, or both.

(3) *Poor balance*. This fault usually goes hand in hand with rushing the kick. Poor balance will result in pulling the ball off line to the left.

(4) *Trying to kick too hard*. When you try to kick too hard, it usually upsets your timing. You end up trying to throw your leg into the ball without the body action that will provide true power. You end up off balance, and even your follow-through is messed up.

I should stress one thing right now. You will make the team by showing the coach that you can kick straight and consistently—not by kicking the ball far once in a while. The coach knows that, if you can show him a nice easy style that keeps the ball on target, distance will eventually take care of itself. Remember, your strength will grow naturally. You have to make sure that your skill grows as well.

5. Moving Out to the Football Field

WHEN YOU are kicking the football with some consistency at a target, you will want to try your new skill on the football field. Go out on the field alone with your kicking tee. This is when the fun of place kicking will really begin. You will be looking at the goal posts and the crossbars; they will be your challenge from that time on.

Tee the ball up between the goal posts on the five-yard line. High school football fields have the goal posts set ten yards back, so your first attempt will be a fifteen-yard kick. You must get enough elevation on the ball to clear the crossbar. Remember that meeting the ball smoothly with the high instep of the foot will give you control and elevation. You are going to find that it is much easier to kick on the football field than it was before, when you were using a tree for a target. I can guarantee that, when you are looking at the crossbar, you will instinctively get your foot under the ball and get it up in the air.

You should work on your short kicks until you are able to get the ball over pretty regularly. Kick from five, ten, fifteen yards out in the beginning. You have to be ready to accept the fact that, at this stage, distance is not yet important. The important thing is getting the ball up over the crossbar and between the uprights.

The next phase you must learn is kicking from an angle. The time to do this is while you are still practicing by yourself with the kicking tee. You will find when you are playing with a team that sixty percent of your attempts will be from the right side of the field. This is because most passers and running backs are right-handed, and, consequently, most plays are run to the right and most passes are thrown to the right.

When you kick from the right or left hashmarks, you will have to make adjustments to your ap-

Here's how my center, holder, and I line up for a kick from the right hashmark.

. . . and here's an attempt from the left side.

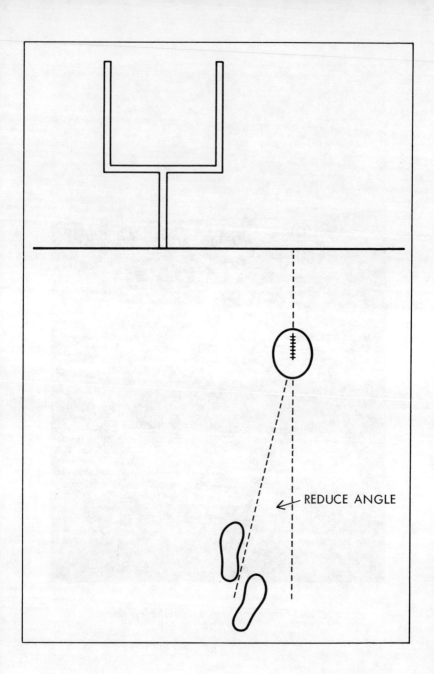

REDUCE ANGLE

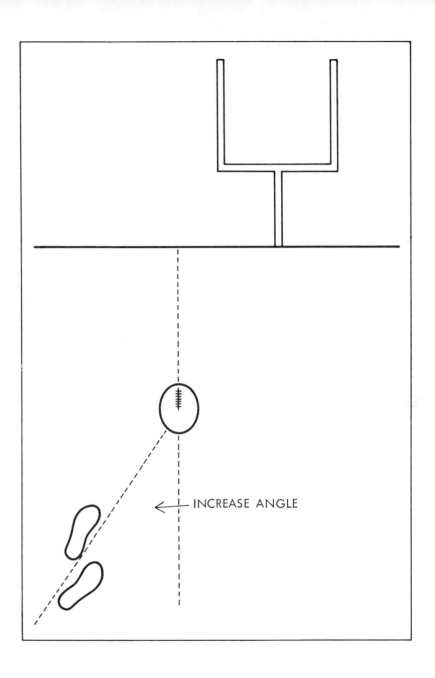

INCREASE ANGLE

proach. The ball is always teed up with the laces facing the goal line . . . not the goal posts. Later on, when you are working with a holder and a center, they will line up over the ball with the holder directly behind the center regardless of whether the goal posts are straight ahead, to the left, or to the right.

When you set up your angle of approach, think of this angle as being based on a straight line from the ball to the goal line. If you are kicking from the right hashmark, your target will be to the left of this line to the goal. By reducing your angle of approach—making it less than thirty degrees—you will be directing the line of flight to the left toward the uprights.

As you would expect, when kicking from the left hashmark, you make the opposite adjustment. You move around to your left, increasing the angle of approach. This changes the line of flight of the ball to the right toward the goal posts. As you practice kicking from different spots on the field, you will become more and more adept at determining the right angle of approach.

KICKOFF

Another phase of the kicking game you should practice on the field is kicking off.

Since you are already accustomed to kicking using a tee, kicking off will present no new problems. Just keep in mind that you are practicing a kick that will be very important in a game. Your kickoff will determine where the opposing team puts the ball in play. A high deep kick will get the ball downfield and also give the men on your kickoff team time to get downfield to cover the runback. Concentration is the key to a good kickoff.

I begin concentrating on the kick the moment I tee the ball up. As I walk back to my starting position, about six yards back, I keep watching the ball. This psyches me up for the kick. I never take my eyes off the ball until it disappears downfield. If you let something distract you or if you let your mind wander, your kick may be affected.

How far back should you stand? It's up to you. Some kickers take a long running start at the ball —as much as twelve to fifteen yards. I feel that

49

Fran Tarkenton has positioned himself on one knee, seven yards behind the center. He looks back to see if I am ready.

Fran extends his hands and waits for the snap from Greg Larson.

He places the ball down and holds it almost perpendicular to the ground with the first finger of his right hand. If necessary, he rotates the ball with his left hand so that the laces face away from the impact area.

I plant my left foot alongside the ball and begin my kicking motion.

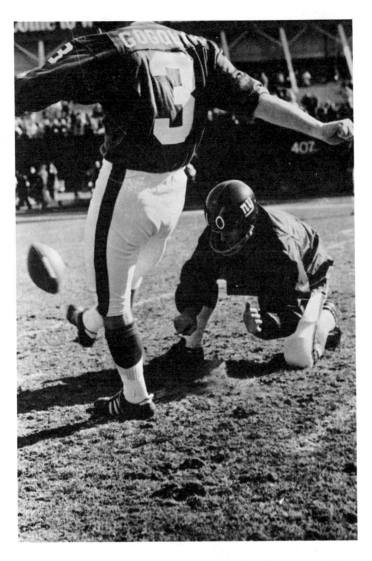

As all good holders do, Tarkenton keeps his fingers in position and his head down well after the kick is away. A premature lifting of either his finger or head could result in the ball moving.

such a long approach gets you running too fast when you reach the ball, which can upset your timing and balance. I recommend that you start from five to six yards behind the ball. Experiment with this a little. Once you determine what distance works well with your natural stride, then you can make that distance part of your standard approach. Soon your steps as you move toward the ball will become automatic. Use the thirty-degree angle of approach.

Even under game conditions, the kickoff is one time when you are not rushed. You can take your time and concentrate on meeting the ball the way you should. Distance is the important factor when you kick off. Accuracy is secondary, as long as you keep the ball on the playing field. In order to get the distance you will be looking for, go back to the fundamentals. Keep your eye on the ball, so you will contact the ball exactly right. Get your body into the kick so that you will deliver maximum power. Follow through. This will help put all of the elements of a good kick together.

Don't practice kicking off too often. This kind

of kicking puts too much strain on your leg. Twice a week—about six or eight kicks each time—should suffice. Your kicking-off practice should be done after extra point and field goal practice to make sure that your leg is sufficiently warmed up.

USING A HOLDER AND CENTER

When you practice alone on the field using the tee, you have all the time you need. You tee the ball up, you get set. Then you kick when you are ready. But you are training yourself to be a place kicker on a football team, and this means working with a center and a holder. That means a new factor to consider—timing. Someday you will be kicking in a game. You will have about a second and a half from the moment the ball is snapped to get your kick away. You can see that this means pretty close timing between the center, your holder, and you, the kicker. Your biggest problem right now is that you probably don't have a center and a holder. You are going to find that your friends want to throw and catch the football. They like to run with it and kick it, but they aren't going to want to center and hold the ball for you. Later on, when you make the team as a place kicker, the coach will assign a center and a holder to work with you. In the meantime, here's what you can do. Get your father, or your brother, or a friend and go out on the football field. You now have a holder. This is a great way to spend an afternoon with your dad; he'll probably enjoy it. If you go out to the field with your father, a brother, or a friend, you can take turns holding and kicking.

The important thing here is to adjust to someone placing the ball on the tee for you and then holding it. The photographs show the proper way for your holder to hold the ball. He should hold it almost straight up and down . . . just tilted back slightly, and, of course, the laces should be pointed away from the point of impact. Now you should practice kicking with your holder from different parts of the field, just as you did before. Remember to adjust your angles when kicking from the left and right hashmarks.

PRACTICING WITH A CENTER

When the time comes to try out for your local team, you will be able to show the coach that you are well on the way to becoming a place kicker. If you can demonstrate to him that you can get the ball over the crossbar regularly from various angles, he will be glad to give you a place on the team. Explain to him that you learned to kick soccer style by using the techniques outlined in this book. Now you will have the opportunity for some practice with a center as well as a holder, so that you can learn to kick under game conditions.

The coach will assign certain players to the kicking unit. The two most important to you will be the holder and the center. It is likely that a quarterback will be selected as your holder. This is because a quarterback handles the ball frequently and therefore has "good hands." He will be able to receive the snap from the center and position the ball for you quickly. Another reason for using a quarterback as a holder is that, in a fake kick situation, he will be able to throw a pass effectively.

It is equally important to have a good center on the kicking unit. He must get off a good crisp snap to your holder, and it must be right on target. Greg Larsen, the New York Giants center, works with me on our kicking unit. Greg really has his snap down to an art. When he centers the ball to my holder, he sends it back in a perfect spiral. Not only is it right on target; it hits the holder's hands with the laces facing up. This means that all he has to do is set the ball down on its nose and the laces will be facing away from the kick area. This can be very important in a game, since I will be trying to get my kick away in 1.2 seconds.

When you begin working with a center and a holder, you will have to establish your own rhythm. First, make sure your holder is lined up directly behind the center, seven yards back. Kicking from either closer to the line of scrimmage or farther back than seven yards results in more blocked kicks. Most kickers will indicate to their holders exactly where they want the ball placed on the ground. Since you will be using a tee for place kicking in high school ball, the holder will position the tee just where you want it.

For a kick, assume your normal stance at a thirty-degree angle from the line of flight of ball to the uprights. Now watch the ball as it is passed back from the center to the holder. Begin your first step the moment your holder puts the ball on the tee. When you see the football touch the tee, rivet your eyes to it and keep them there throughout your approach, kick, and follow-through. Hopefully, you will see it sailing through the uprights.

Now that you have a regular kicking unit, you should practice working with them as much as possible. It is important to practice from various distances and from both sides of the field. When kicking from either left or right angles, have your holder line up directly behind the center as he would for a straightaway kick. Show him where you want the tee placed on the ground and then determine what the line of flight must be for the

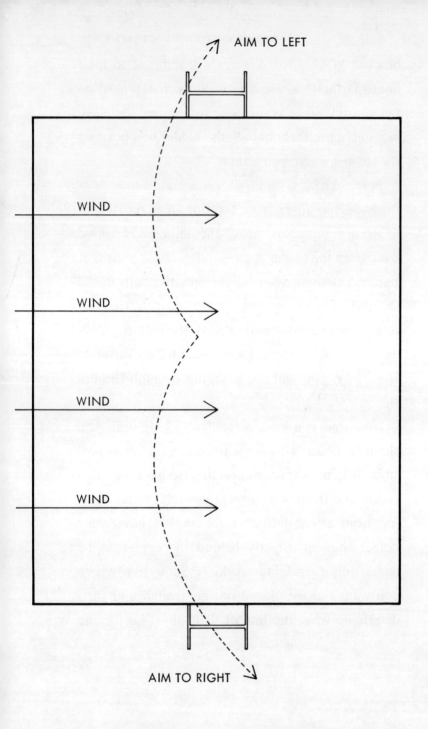

ball to split the uprights. You can now set up your angle of approach—less than thirty degrees for a kick from the right, more than thirty degrees for a kick from the left.

During these practice sessions you will be encountering the varying wind conditions that you will experience later in your games. This is the time to learn how cross winds and headwinds will effect your kicks. When you understand how the wind effects the flight of the ball, you can make the appropriate adjustments. I can't give you any rules or formulas to follow, since the conditions under which you will be kicking will be always changing. The distances will differ, the angles will differ, the intensity and direction of the wind will differ. This is why a kicker takes a few practice kicks at each end of the field before a game. He notes how the wind affects his straightaway kicks and his kicks from the hashmarks. If there is a cross wind, for example, the kicker may have to aim a bit to the right at one end of the field and compensate to the left at the other end.

Your practice sessions with your center and holder are truly important. The three of you are getting ready to add a vital weapon to your team's offense. One of these days now you will be called upon to do your thing in a game. And I know you will want to deliver that three-point score.

6. Kicking Under Game Conditions

WHEN YOUR team is playing a game, your relationship to the game will be somewhat different from that of your teammates. First of all, since you are a specialist, your job doesn't coincide with that of anyone else on the team. When the defensive team comes off the field, the linemen will group together and discuss the blocking that is being used against them. The defensive backs will exchange information on the opposing team's pass patterns. Your quarterback, receivers, and running backs will have plenty to talk about when the defensive unit is on the field.

As a place kicker, you always have to be ready to go into the game. I know that in any given game I may never get a shot at a field goal; but, if I get one, I'm ready. I begin to prepare for my possible chance at a field goal before the game starts. Before I suit up for the game, I go out on the field, especially if it is a strange field. I check the surface of the field, which tells me what kind of football shoes to wear. If the field is muddy or especially soft, I will be sure to have extra-long cleats on my left shoe. A flag or pennant can tell you the direction and strength of the wind. A cross wind means that I will have to aim either to the right or left of the uprights to compensate. A strong headwind means that I will be kicking as hard as I can. During the 1971 season, we were playing the Steelers at Pittsburgh Stadium. We were four points behind with about five minutes left when I was sent in to try a thirty-seven-yard field goal. There was a tremendous headwind blowing from the left, and on top of that it was bitter cold and snowing. I kicked the ball as hard as I could from the right hashmark. The distance was okay, but I just missed the right upright. Even though I missed, I learned something; you have to learn from your misses as well as from your successful attempts.

When the game starts, I go down to the end of

the bench and follow things alone. It's not that I'm aloof from my teammates. It's just that my job has to be done alone, and I can better prepare for it if I keep to myself. On a cold day, I often run back and forth near the sidelines to keep my leg warmed up and ready. A long field goal can make severe demands on your kicking muscles and a cold leg just may not do the job. If I see that our offense may be approaching a fourth down situation within field goal range, I get myself ready. Here's how:

First, I check the position of the ball on the field. Will a possible field goal attempt be made from the center of the field or at a slight angle to the left or maybe from the right hashmark? Will the wind be a factor? How much of a factor? Once I analyze these elements, I pick out a spot on the ground—maybe a piece of paper or a tuft of grass. This is the time I set up my approach. I figure my angle, taking the wind into consideration. Next I actually practice my kicking motion, using my imaginary ball on the ground. It is also important to observe what yard line the ball is on, remembering that you will be kicking from seven yards back. Now, if the coach calls for the kicking unit,

HERE'S WHAT A KICK FROM THE
RIGHT HASHMARK LOOKS LIKE
FROM BEHIND:

*I lean forward as I prepare to
take my first step. The first step
is with my right foot.*

*Going into the second step,
both feet are off the ground.
My right foot is cocked back.*

*As my right foot drives through
the ball, I still have my head
down and my eyes on the spot
where the ball was teed up.*

The ball is away and I follow through.

I can go out on the field knowing exactly where I want the ball placed and what angle of approach to use. Since you will be using a place kicking tee, you can put the tee down where you want it before your kicking team huddles up.

After the huddle breaks, move right back to your kicking position. You should be confident and deliberate as you assume your stance. You may also be nervous. This is a good sign. It means your body is peaked up for its job. It also means that you are concerned about what you are doing and want to do it right. I think that any place kicker who isn't a little nervous before kicking doesn't really belong on a team. You'll find that once you get into position the nervousness fades away. Another feeling comes into focus now—concentration!

This is the key to place kicking under game conditions: concentrate! Concentrate! Keep your attention on the things that are important to your place kicking attempt. Watch your center, your holder's hands—these are familiar to you from your many hours of practice together. Try not to think of the opposing team. And very important—

don't look up as the defensive linemen charge in to try to block the kick. Keep your eye on the ball and try to treat this kick as though it were just another routine practice kick. Be loose, get your body into the kick, and follow through. Those three important points on the scoreboard will be reward enough for all the practice, the work, and the pressure.

Here's one last thought about kicking in a game. If you miss one, don't let it get you down. Of course, you will be disappointed. But remember, the guys on the team will be counting on you to make the next one. You have to be up and ready the next time your team is in field goal position. That's what you have to be thinking about—your next kick—not your last one.

Here I am kicking an extra point against the Colts.

7. Conventional Place Kicking

IN CASE you find that you just can't seem to adjust to the soccer-style kick, I am going to give you several pointers on conventional place kicking. If you decide that conventional kicking is easier for you, you will find that there are two advantages in using this method. One, you will be able to find more coaches that were raised on conventional kicking. They will be able to give more coaching in this style of kicking than in soccer style. Second, if you have to rely on books such as this one to learn the fundamentals, there has been a lot more material written about conventional kicking than there has been about soccer style.

I will point out the ways in which the two techniques are similar. This will help assure you that your efforts up until now have not been wasted. Certainly everything that I have told you about training and conditioning applies whether you are going to kick soccer or conventional style. Being relaxed and concentration are important no matter what kicking method you use. Another thing that is vitally important to all place kickers is keeping the eyes glued to the ball throughout the kick.

Two factors are going to tempt you to take your eyes off the ball prematurely. One is the thundering hoofbeats of the charging defensive linemen. They want to distract you or block the kick if possible. You have to learn to live with defensive linemen if you are going to be a place kicker. Second, you will sometimes tend to look up in anticipation of seeing the ball sail through the uprights. If you look too soon—that is, before your foot drives through the ball—it probably won't sail between the uprights at all. Looking up too soon will throw your kick off completely.

Finally, the follow-through is just as important a part of the straightaway kick as it is in the soccer kick. From here on, you will be doing everything differently:

THE STANCE

You can forget about that thirty-degree angle now. Position yourself directly behind the ball. An imaginary line should run from your position, through the ball, and straight to the target. How far back should you stand? Well, in observing conventional place kickers, I've noticed that, while they all seem to use a two-step approach—right, left, kick—some prefer to start with a short half step with the right foot. Other kickers take a full step with the right, or full step with the left, and then kick with the right foot. I think you will have to experiment a little to find your natural stride. As before, set up in a relaxed position, bent forward slightly at the waist, with your arms hanging loosely at your sides.

THE APPROACH

Your approach in straightaway kicking is simplified because you no longer have to concern yourself with angles. Once again, rivet your eyes to the ball. Step off with your right foot. The next step with your left foot is crucial. It will affect the height of the kick, the distance, and the direction. Ideally, your left foot should plant itself firmly on the ground about three inches to the left of the ball and about six inches behind it. It should be pointed straight at your target, since you don't want any rotating hip action on a conventional kick. Pointing your left foot to the left or right of the intended line of flight of the ball will cause this adverse hip action and send your kick off line. Most kickers extend their arms out for balance as they cock the right leg back.

THE KICK

Probably the biggest difference between soccer-style kicking and conventional style is the point of impact on the foot. For straightaway kicking you contact the ball with your toe—not the high in-step. This means that the tip of your foot must be made into a firm tool for contacting the ball. You do this by turning your toes up in your special kick-

The Giants try to block an attempt by Baltimore's conventional-style kicker Jim O'Brien.

ing shoe and locking your ankle. If you don't lock your ankle, your foot will give with the impact as it strikes the ball, and this movement of your foot will absorb power from your kick and upset its directional control.

To get maximum power from a straightaway kick, drive your right foot through the ball. As your foot approaches the impact area, bend your left knee slightly. You should have the feeling that you are getting the seat of your pants into the kick. This gets body action as well as leg action into your kick. Follow through by bringing your leg straight up toward your target.

8. The Appeal of Soccer

EARLIER in this book I briefly mentioned some reasons why playing soccer can be valuable to the place kicker. In addition to being about the best way to get your legs in shape for kicking, you will find that soccer is fun. It's a great game, and here's why. If you are training yourself to be a place kicker, you are becoming a specialist. This means that as a kicking specialist you will be playing only for a minute or so in each game. You have already decided that these brief opportunities are rewarding enough to compensate for all the long hours of work and practice. But when you play soccer, you find that you are really a part of the game—all the way, with both offensive and defensive responsibilities. Soccer allows you, the football specialist, to become an all-around player in another exciting sport.

Many of the reasons why you chose to become a kicker in football will also cause soccer to appeal to you. A soccer player does not have to be unusually big or strong, or even exceptionally fast. He must be alert and agile and have endurance. The same principles that help you to become a good place kicker will turn you into a good soccer player. These principles are: developing good techniques and getting plenty of practice until you are competent in these techniques.

In football, most of the action is built around plays that are designed by the coaching staff. These plays are presented on the blackboard, run over and over on the practice field, then used at the right time in a game. Each play is a brief flurry of action beginning with the snap of the ball and ending—several seconds later—when the ball is blown dead. Soccer is somewhat similar to basketball and hockey in that the action between goals is continuous. Teams work off basic patterns but do not use plays in the sense that we, as football players, think of plays. Soccer is more a game of player pitted against player, using his instincts, his reactions, his skills to make the most of situations as they occur in the game. Soccer is a fast-paced sport that gives the player many opportunities to use the techniques that he is continually practicing: tricky head shots, a variety of kicks and passes, traps, tackles, dribbles, and the all-important try for goal.

You can see that this is not a game for the specialist. You also can see that this is not a game in which the big, powerful player has an advantage over the smaller, agile boy. In fact, agility and the ability to outguess your opponent will make you a much more effective soccer player than will size or strength.

Once you have been exposed to soccer, you will understand why it is probably the world's favorite sport. Ancient records tell us that kicking games resembling soccer were played in places such as Greece, Rome, and China thousands of years ago. History reveals that centuries ago in Europe people played a game that most likely grew to be our modern game of soccer. Try to imagine hordes of people from one village attempting to move an air-filled bladder to the next village (the goal). The folks from town number two would be the defensive team—unless the ball changed hands. Such a game may have lasted all day and involved scores of players. That was a soccer game of five hundred years ago. Over the years the game became more organized. Contests were held on designated playing areas rather than chasing the ball from village to village. Then, in the nineteenth century, some universal rules were adopted. At that point, international competition became possible.

9. Soccer Fundamentals

I AM PUTTING a soccer section in this book because I want you to give soccer a try. I want you to share this experience that boys and men all over the world are enjoying. Who knows? . . . Maybe someday you'll be playing in an international match.

I will introduce you to some fundamental soccer techniques—passing, trapping, tackling, heading, dribbling. These are the tools of the soccer player, and you must be able to handle them just to step on a soccer field. I will not attempt to cover complicated offensive and defensive maneuvers and team play, since these will come later, when you are on a team. There are some excellent books on

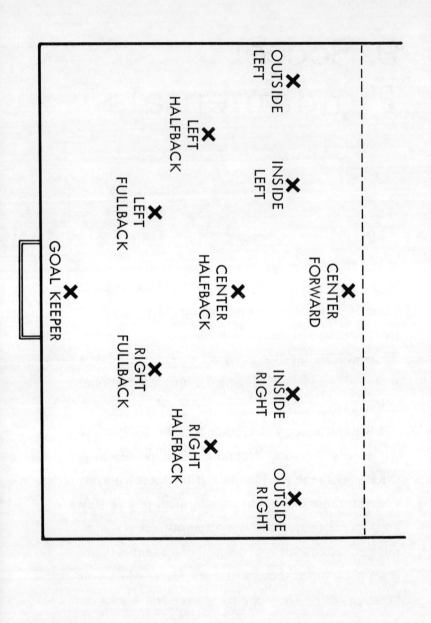

soccer that can help you and your soccer buddies develop a winning team. Right now I want to help you to make a team.

What makes a soccer team? Just like a football team, a soccer team has eleven men. But the resemblance ends right there. Each side has a goal keeper, two fullbacks, three halfbacks, and five forwards. Here's a diagram of the way the players line up.

There is a left fullback, a right fullback, a left half, a center half, and a right half. The forwards are designated as outside right, outside left, inside right, inside left, and center forward.

To play soccer all you really need is a soccer ball and an open area to use for a playing field. There is only one piece of equipment that is important—a fitted pair of soccer boots. I want to emphasize the word *fitted*. In order to protect your feet from injuries and blisters, as well as to help the accuracy of your kicks, your boots must fit perfectly. They should be a little on the snug side. If you are lucky enough to be on a soccer team, your coach will be able to advise you on selecting the right boots. The rest of the soccer uniform consists of a jersey, short pants, and a pair of soccer stockings. I expect that you will improvise somewhat on these items. Most soccer players wear shin guards under their stockings. This is a good idea in view of all the kicking that goes on at close quarters in a soccer game. Put your new soccer boots on, get your soccer ball, and we'll begin.

TRAPPING THE BALL

Trapping the soccer ball means bringing it under your control when it is bouncing in flight or rolling. Trapping is done to make it possible to kick the ball yourself or pass it immediately.

The simplest way to trap the ball is to smother it with your foot as it approaches you. More difficult trapping is done with the chest or with the knees in combination with the feet. A skilled soccer player can catch a ball in flight with the inside of his foot, bring the ball to the ground, and be off with it under full control.

84

KICKING

If you have been able to develop some proficiency at kicking the football soccer style, you shouldn't have much trouble kicking the soccer ball. Remember to plant your left foot alongside the ball parallel to the line of flight. Swing your leg through the ball, contacting it with the high instep. Keep your eye on the ball throughout the entire kick and then follow through. Don't forget to get your body into the kick in order to achieve distance.

To pass the ball, the inside of the foot is used. A pass to the left is made with the inside of the right foot. As in kicking for distance, it is important that the toe of your kicking foot be extended, not bent at the ankle. Learning to kick and pass the soccer ball will require a great deal of practice. When you practice, make sure that you develop your skills with both feet. A soccer player must be able to pass just as accurately with his left foot as with his right. He also must be able to kick with power using either foot.

The goalkeeper is the only man on a soccer team who may use his hands. The Cosmos' goalkeeper shows some spectacular examples of typical "saves."

Trapping the ball with the foot.

This man traps the ball with his body.

HEADING THE BALL

Soccer players often pass the ball to a teammate by using their foreheads. This is called "heading the ball." I have found that some beginners at soccer are afraid that the ball striking the head will hurt. This causes them to blink their eyes at the moment of contact. You can't head the ball with your eyes closed. My advice is to begin with a light ball—like a beach ball.

Ask your father or a friend to throw the beach ball to you. Keep your eyes open and allow the ball to strike your forehead above your eyes, right about at your hairline. The light ball won't hurt a bit, especially if you contact it with this proper part of your head. As the ball strikes your forehead, look back toward your friend and make a little nodding motion of your head. The ball will bounce right back to him. The nodding motion is important because it establishes the fact that you are hitting the ball with your head rather than merely allowing the ball to hit you.

Now that you are able to head the beach ball

To head the ball correctly, use the forehead, just below the hairline.

without flinching try using your soccer ball. You will find that, although the soccer ball is heavier, it won't hurt you if you meet it with your forehead. After a while, your neck muscles will gain strength and you will be able to get power and direction behind the ball. Your coach will show you exercises that will strengthen the neck muscles used in heading the soccer ball.

DRIBBLING

The soccer player advances the ball with his feet by a means of a succession of light kicks. This is called dribbling. The toe of your shoe is not used to dribble the ball; rather, the inside and outside of your foot are employed. Many beginnners at soccer find dribbling with the insides of the feet to be easier than using the outsides. Don't make this mistake. Using just the insides of your feet will get you by for a while; but if you ever want to become a good soccer player, you must be able to control the ball with both the insides and outsides of the feet.

92

*A skillful dribbler can move the ball with both the insides and
outsides of his feet.*

If you have an opportunity to watch good soccer players in action, give special attention to the dribbling. You will notice that the best dribblers keep their bodies loose—hips, legs, ankles. This gives them dexterity and the ability to change direction quickly without losing control of the ball. When you practice dribbling, keep this in mind. Don't stand too erect. Lean forward slightly from the waist. Keep your arms loose as well as the rest of your joints. As you become adept at controlling the ball with your feet, practice making quick cuts and changes of direction. If you can keep the ball close to your feet, you will develop a high degree of mobility and control.

TACKLING

Tackling in soccer means going in and taking the ball from your opponent or causing him to loose or surrender control of the ball. You do this by driving into the ball with your body either from the front or the side of your opponent. Drive in hard, digging your shoulder into the man with the

Tackling, in soccer, means taking the ball away from your opponent.

ball. It won't do just to use one leg to try to take the ball away from your man. He will sweep right by you. Go in hard and come away with the ball.

10. Soccer Rules

STANDARDIZED rules of soccer are followed all over the world and make international competition possible. Through the courtesy of the North American Soccer League, I am providing the following summary of rules from the United States Football Association rulebook.

LAWS OF THE GAME

THE FIELD OF PLAY

Dimensions. The field of play shall be rectangular, its length being not more than 130 yards nor less than 100 yards and its breadth not more than

100 yards nor less than 50 yards. (In International Matches the length shall be not more than 120 yards nor less than 110 yards and the breadth not more than 80 yards nor less than 70 yards.) The length shall in all cases exceed the breadth.

The goal area. At each end of the field of play two lines shall be drawn at right angles to the goal line, 6 yards from each goal post. These shall extend into the field of play for a distance of 6 yards and shall be joined by a line drawn parallel with the goal line. Each of the spaces enclosed by these lines and the goal line shall be called a goal area.

The penalty area. At each end of the field of play two lines shall be drawn at right angles to the goal line, 18 yards from each goal post. These shall extend into the field of play for a distance of 18 yards and shall be joined by a line drawn parallel with the goal line. Each of the spaces enclosed by these lines and the goal line shall be called a penalty area. A suitable mark shall be made within each penalty area, 12 yards from the mid-point of the goal line, measured along an undrawn line at right angles thereto. These shall be the penalty-kick marks. From each penalty-kick mark an arc of a circle, having a radius of 10 yards, shall be drawn outside the penalty area.

The corner area. From each corner flagpost a quarter circle, having a radius of 1 yard, shall be drawn inside the field of play.

The goals. The goals shall be placed on the center of each goal line and shall consist of two upright posts, equidistant from the corner flags and 8 yards apart (inside measurement), joined by a horizontal crossbar the lower edge of which shall be 8 feet from the ground. The width and depth of the goal posts and the width and depth of the crossbars shall not exceed 5 inches.

Nets may be attached to the posts, crossbars, and grounded behind the goals. They should be appropriately supported and be so placed as to allow the goalkeeper ample room.

DURATION OF THE GAME

The duration of the game shall be two equal periods of 45 minutes, unless otherwise mutually agreed upon, subject to the following: (a) Allowance shall be made in either period for all time lost through accident or other cause, the amount of which shall be a matter for the discretion of the Referee; (b) Time shall be extended to permit of a penalty kick being taken at or after the expiration of the normal period in either half.

At half-time the interval shall not exceed five minutes except by consent of the Referee.

THE START OF PLAY

(*a*) *At the beginning of the game,* choice of ends and the kickoff shall be decided by the toss of a coin. The team winning the toss shall have the option of choice of ends or the kickoff.

The Referee having given a signal, the game shall be started by a player taking a place kick (i.e., a kick at the ball while it is stationary on the ground in the center of the field of play) into his opponents' half of the field of play. Every player shall be in his own half of the field and every player of the team opposing that of the kicker shall remain not less than 10 yards from the ball until it is kicked off; it shall not be deemed in play until it has traveled the distance of its own circumference. The kicker shall not play the ball a second time until it has been played or touched by another player.

(*b*) *After a goal has been scored,* the game shall be restarted in like manner by a player of the team losing the goal.

(*c*) *After half-time;* when restarting after half-time, ends shall be changed and the kickoff shall be taken by a player of the opposite team to that of the player who started the game.

Punishment. For any infringement of this Law, the kickoff shall be retaken, except in the case of the kicker playing the ball again before it has been touched or played by another player; for this offense, an indirect free kick shall be taken by a player of the opposing team from the place where the infringement occurred. A goal shall not be scored direct from a kickoff.

(*d*) *After any other temporary suspension;* when restarting the game after a temporary suspension of play from any cause not mentioned elsewhere in these Laws, provided that immediately prior to the suspension the ball has not passed over the touch or goal lines, the Referee shall drop the ball at the place where it was when play was suspended and it shall be deemed in play when it has touched the ground; if, however, it goes over the touch or goal lines after it has been dropped by the Referee, but before it is touched by a player, the Referee shall again drop it. A player shall not play the ball until it has touched the ground. If this section of the Law is not complied with the Referee shall again drop the ball.

BALL IN AND OUT OF PLAY

The ball is out of play:

(a) When it has wholly crossed the goal line or touch line, whether on the ground or in the air.

(b) When the game has been stopped by the Referee.

The ball is in play at all other times from the start of the match to the finish including:

(a) If it rebounds from a goal post, crossbar, or corner flagpost into the field of play.

(b) If it rebounds off either the Referee or Linesmen when they are in the field of play.

(c) In the event of a supposed infringement of the Laws, until a decision is given.

METHOD OF SCORING

Except as otherwise provided by these Laws, a goal shall be scored when the whole of the ball has passed over the goal line, between the goal posts and under the crossbar, provided it has not been thrown, carried or propelled by hand or arm, by a player of the attacking side. Should the crossbar become displaced for any reason during the game, and the ball cross the goal line at a point which, in the opinion of the Referee, is below where the crossbar should have been, he shall award a goal.

The team scoring the greater number of goals during a game shall be the winner; if no goals, or an equal number of goals are scored, the game shall be termed a "draw" (tie).

OFF-SIDE

A player is off-side if he is nearer his opponents' goal line than the ball *at the moment the ball is played unless:*

(a) He is in his own half of the field of play.

(b) There are two of his opponents nearer to their own goal line than he is.

(c) *The ball last touched an opponent or was last played by him.*

(d) He receives the ball direct from a goal kick, a corner kick, a throw-in, or when it is dropped by the Referee.

Punishment. For an infringement of this Law, an indirect free kick shall be taken by a player of the opposing team from the place where the infringement occurred.

A player in an off-side position shall not be penalized unless, in the opinion of the Referee, he is interfering with the play or with an opponent, or is seeking to gain an advantage by being in an offside position.

FOULS AND MISCONDUCT

1. A player who intentionally commits any of the following nine offenses:

(a)   Kicks or attempts to kick an opponent;

(b)   Trips an opponent, i.e., throwing or attempting to throw him by use of the legs or by stooping in front of or behind him;

(c)   Jumps at an opponent;

(d)   Charges an opponent in a violent or dangerous manner;

(e)   Charges an opponent from behind unless the latter be obstructing;

(f)   Strikes or attempts to strike an opponent;

(g)   Holds an opponent with his hand or any part of his arm;

(h)   Pushes an opponent with his hand or any part of his arm;

(i)   Handles the ball, i.e., carries, strikes or

propels the ball with his hand or arm (this does not apply to the goalkeeper within his own penalty area) shall be penalized by the award of a direct free kick to be taken by the opposing side from the place where the offense occurred.

Should a player of the defending side intentionally commit one of the above nine offenses within the penalty area he shall be penalized by a *penalty kick*. A penalty kick can be awarded irrespective of the position of the ball, if in play, at the time an offense within the penalty area is committed.

2. *A player committing any of the five following offenses:*

1. Playing in a manner considered by the Referee to be dangerous, e.g., attempting to kick the ball while held by the goalkeeper;

2. Charging fairly, i.e., with the shoulder, when the ball is not within playing distance of the players concerned and they are definitely not trying to play it;

3. When not playing the ball, intentionally obstructing an opponent, i.e., running between an opponent and the ball, or interposing

the body as to form an obstacle to an opponent.

4. Charging the goalkeeper except when he—

   (a) is holding the ball

   (b) is obstructing an opponent

   (c) has passed outside his goal area;

5. When playing as a goalkeeper: (a) takes more than four steps while holding, bouncing or throwing the ball in the air and catching it again without releasing it so that it is played by another player, or

   (b) indulges in tactics which, in the opinion of the Referee, are designed merely to hold up the game and thus waste time and so give an unfair advantage to his own team, shall be penalized by the award of an indirect free kick to be taken by the opposing side from the place where the infringement occurred.

3. A player shall be cautioned if:

(j) He enters the field of play to join or rejoin his team after the game has commenced without first having received a signal from the Referee showing him that he is ordered to do so. (This clause is not applicable in the case of Law 4.)

If the game has been stopped (to administer the caution) it shall be restarted by the Referee dropping the ball at the place where the infringement occurred, but if the player has committed a more important offense he shall be penalized according to that section of the law infringed:

(k) He persistently infringes the Laws of the Game;

(l) He shows by word or action dissent from any decision given by the Referee;

(m) He is guilty of ungentlemanly conduct;

For any of these last three offenses, in addition to the caution, *an indirect free kick* shall also be awarded to the opposing side from the place where the offense occurred.

4. A player shall be sent off the field of play if he

1. Persists in misconduct after having received a caution.

2. Is guilty of violent conduct, i.e., using foul or abusive language, or if, in the opinion of the Referee, he is guilty of serious foul play.

If play be stopped by reason of a player being

ordered from the field for an offense without a separate breach of the Law having been committed, the game shall be resumed by an indirect free kick to be taken by a player of the opposing team from the place where the infringement occurred.

FREE KICK

Free kicks shall be classified under two heads: "direct" (from which a goal can be scored direct against the offending side), and "indirect" (from which a goal cannot be scored unless the ball has been played or touched by a player other than the kicker before passing through the goal).

When a player is taking a direct or indirect free kick inside his own penalty area, all of the opposing players shall remain outside the area, and shall be at least ten yards from the ball while the kick is being taken. The ball shall be in play immediately when it has traveled the distance of its own circumference and is beyond the penalty area. The goalkeeper shall not receive the ball into his hands, in order that he may thereafter kick it into play. If the ball is not kicked direct into play, beyond the penalty area, the kick shall be retaken.

When a player is taking a direct or indirect free kick outside his own penalty area, all of the opposing players shall be at least ten yards from the ball, until it is in play, unless they are standing on their own goal line, between the goal posts. The ball shall be in play when it has traveled the distance of its own circumference.

If a player of the opposing side encroaches into the penalty area, or within ten yards of the ball, as the case may be, before a free kick is taken, the Referee shall delay the taking of the kick, until the law is complied with.

The ball must be stationary when a free kick is taken, and the kicker shall not play the ball a second time until it has been touched or played by another player.

PENALTY KICK

A penalty kick shall be taken from the penalty

mark and, when it is being taken, all players, with the exception of the player taking the kick, and the opposing goalkeeper, shall be within the field of play but outside the penalty area, and at least 10 yards from the penalty mark. The opposing goalkeeper must stand (without moving his feet) on his own goal line, between the goal posts, until the ball is kicked. The player taking the kick must kick the ball forward; he shall not play the ball a second time until it has been touched or played by another player. The ball shall be deemed in play directly it is kicked, i.e., traveled the distance of its circumference, and a goal may be scored direct from such a penalty kick. If the ball touches the goalkeeper before passing between the posts, when a penalty kick is being taken at or after the expiration of half-time or full-time, it does not nullify a goal. If necessary, time of play shall be extended at half-time or full-time to allow a penalty kick to be taken.

Punishment: (a) For any infringement by the defending team the kick shall be retaken, if a goal has not resulted.

(b) For any infringement by the attacking

team, other than by the player taking the kick, *if a goal is scored by this player the goal shall be disallowed and the kick retaken.*

(c) For any infringement by the player taking the penalty-kick, a player of the opposing team shall take an indirect free kick from the spot where the infringement occurred.

THROW-IN

When the whole of the ball passes over a touch-line, either on the ground or in the air, it shall be thrown in from the point where it crossed the line, in any direction, by a player of the team opposite to that of the player who last touched it. The thrower at the moment of delivering the ball must face the field of play and part of each foot shall be either *on the touch-line* or *on the ground* outside the touch-line. The thrower shall use both hands and shall deliver the ball from *behind and over his head.* The ball shall be in play immediately *after it enters the field of play,* but the thrower shall not again play the ball until it has been touched or played by another player. A goal shall not be scored direct from a throw-in.

Punishment: (a) If the ball is improperly thrown in the throw-in shall be taken by a player of the opposing team.

(b) If the thrower plays the ball a second time before it has been touched or played by another player, an indirect free kick shall be taken by a player of the opposing team from the place where the infringement occurred.

GOAL KICK

When the whole of the ball passes over the goal line excluding that portion between the goal posts, either in the air or on the ground, having last been played by one of the attacking team, it shall be kicked direct into play beyond the penalty area, from a point within that half of the goal area nearest to where it crossed the line, by a player of the defending team. A goalkeeper shall not receive the ball into his hands from a goal kick in order that he may thereafter kick it into play. If the ball is not kicked beyond the penalty area, i.e., direct into play, the kick shall be retaken. *The kicker shall not play the ball a second time until it has touched or been played by another player.* A goal shall not be scored direct from such a kick. Players of the team opposing that of the player taking the goal kick shall remain outside the penalty area whilst the kick is being taken.

Punishment: If a player taking a goal kick plays the ball a second time after it has passed beyond the penalty area, but before it has touched or been played by another player, an indirect free kick shall be awarded to the opposing team, to be taken from the place where the infringement occurred.

CORNER KICK

When the whole of the ball passes over the goal line, excluding that portion between the goal posts, either in the air or on the ground, having last been played by one of the defending team, a member of the attacking team shall kick the ball from within the quarter-circle at the nearest corner flagpost, which must not be moved, i.e., a corner kick. A goal may be scored direct from such a kick. Players of the team opposing that of the player taking the corner kick shall not approach within 10 yards of the ball until it is in play, i.e., it has traveled the distance of its own circumference, nor shall the kicker play the ball a second time until it has been touched or played by another player.

Punishment: For an infringement of this Law, an indirect free kick shall be awarded to the opposing team, to be taken from the place where the infringement occurred.

11. Putting It All Together

NOT TOO LONG AGO, place kicking was a part-time job, even in professional football. Kickers were linemen, receivers, or running backs who could also kick a football. For example, Lou Michaels, an active pro place kicker who happens to be among the top ten lifetime scores with the N.F.L., was for many years a fine defensive end. Now that coaches are aware of the value of specialists such as place kickers, they no longer risk these individuals in other assignments. The place kicker on a professional football team is likely to be the team's top scorer.

Now that you have completed the instructions in this book and have become—I hope—a fledgling place kicker, you will be especially interested in the accomplishments of the leading kickers. I have selected one segment of professional football —the Super Bowl—to demonstrate the importance of your new skill. In the 1968 Super Bowl a place kicker made the headlines. In Green Bay's 33-to-14 win over the Oakland Raiders in 1968, Don Chandler of the Packers put four field goals through the uprights out of four attempts. Don kicked placements of thirty-nine, twenty, forty-three and thirty-five yards. Now that's really kicking.

Remember the 1969 Super Bowl . . . the one in which the New York Jets beat the Colts 16 to 7? The Jets pulled one of the great upsets in recent years in that game. And guess who scored most of the points—Jim Turner, New York's field goal specialist. Jim had a great game—three field goals of thirty-two, thirty and nine yards. Turner accounted for ten of the Jet's sixteen points.

When the Kansas City Chiefs got a second shot at a Super Bowl Championship against the Vikings in 1970, they had a potent addition to their offensive arsenal, an exciting soccer-style kicker named Jon Stenarud. Once again, the place kicker stole the show. Jon scored with placements of forty-eight, thirty-two and twenty-five yards.

In 1971 the Baltimore Colts earned a chance to redeem their previous Super Bowl loss to the Jets. They met the Dallas Cowboys at Orange Bowl Stadium in Miami. The teams were well matched and fought to a 13-to-13 tie with the clock running out. It was the dream situation for a place kicker. Jim O'Brien, Baltimore's rookie kicker, came out on the field with five seconds left to play. More than a game was at stake; this was for the World Championship! The ball was snapped, and young O'Brien sent a thirty-two-yard kick spinning through the uprights. A field goal had made the Colts the new Super Bowl Champs!

The supreme thrill that I experience as an athlete occurs in a tied game. This is the thrill I want to share with you—a fellow place kicker. Some crisp autumn afternoon you will watch your team move the ball into field goal range. It's fourth down, with only three seconds left on the clock. The score is tied. Only you can save the game for your team. Only you can turn that tie into a win. That's the time you will know what it's all about

. . . when you put it all together. As the ball sails through the uprights, you will experience that unique thrill—the thrill that has motivated countless athletes to push themselves to their limits to be the best at what they do.

PETE GOGOLAK

Pete Gogolak, who came with his family from Hungary in 1956, is the place kicker for the New York Giants. He was the first player to introduce soccer-style kicking to the game of American football—first as a college player with Cornell, then as a professional. Consistently rated among the top scorers in professional football, he holds the Giants' distance record for field goals, at fifty-four yards.

RAY SIEGENER

Ray Siegener is the author of several books on sports. He has worked with sports figures such as Kyle Rote, Vince Lombardi, and Red Holzman.